Jess Green is a performance poe
performed at Glastonbury, Latitude,
Fringe. Her first collection, Burni
Burning Eye Books was shortlisted fc
Award and as a poetry and music sho ___ ___ reviews at
the Edinburgh Fringe and on its national tour. A poem from
this show, Dear Mr Gove received viral attention on Youtube
in 2014 and has now received over 300,000 views. The theatre
adaptation of Burning Books was longlisted for the Bread &
Roses Theatre Award 2016 and performed to sell-out audiences
at Curve Theatre in Leicester. Burning Books tours nationally
Autumn 2018. Her second poetry and music show, A Self Help
Guide To Being In Love With Jeremy Corbyn based around
her second collection of the same name and performed with
her band, The Mischief Thieves goes to the Edinburgh Fringe
in 2018. Jess has written for Channel 4 and the BBC and
runs Leicester poetry night, Find The Right Words which was
shortlisted for Best Regular UK Poetry Event in the Saboteur
Awards.

Sept '19

To John Kingston

Huge good luck to you!
Stayhopef1

Jess x

A SELF HELP GUIDE
to being **in love** with

JEREMY CORBYN

JESS GREEN

Burning Eye

This edition published by Burning Eye Books 2018

www.burningeye.co.uk

@burningeyebooks

Burning Eye Books
15 West Hill, Portishead, BS20 6LG

ISBN 978-1-91157047-9

Printed & bound by ImprintDigital.com, UK

A Self-Help Guide to Being in Love with Jeremy Corbyn

CONTENTS

A PARTY ON ITS KNEES

We're so accustomed to the disappointment,
the apologies,
yes, but...
membership cards kept to the back of our wallets,
all the mornings we vow over *BBC Breakfast*
enough is enough,
welfare,
workfare,
the anti-immigration mug,
can't keep finding excuses for
academies,
Teach First,
the introduction of tuition fees,
can't keep arguing with the armchair apathy
of our nans
they're all the bloody same,
PFI,
war crimes,
zero-hour contracts,
all the blood he's got on his hands,
clause IV,
Iraq war,
they didn't give two hoots about the bedroom tax.

Then another night of crushing defeat,
the drive to work spent listening
to the list of lost seats,
within a week
another leadership election line-up,
carbon copy cut-out hopefuls,
we've been here before,
we must be tough on
benefit claimants,
we must be tough on
illegal immigrants,
we must be tough on
union power.

In the dying minutes
a soft voice
from the back of the chamber,
mad geriatric,
probably won't even make it on to the nomination paper.

A LOVE LETTER TO JEREMY CORBYN

August 2015

Sun reporters are not sleeping.
They're hairless,
wild-eyed, lip-bitten and greying,
'cause since the downfall
of Lord Sewel,
all screwed up and used up,
all belly and bra straps,
they're desperate to find
someone else to pin up
with their arse out.

They've set their sights on Corbyn
to crush him like a moth under fist,
present him as this
mad, withering, Stalinesque geriatric.

They've paid
every secret source they know
to find one account of him
being corrupted,
but after weeks of rummaging
through the internet
all they've managed
is one mention of Hamas
and £5.60 for an ink cartridge.

Each satirical cartoon
depicting him a dangerous lefty loon
and Tony Blair threatening to rip out
the heart of every voter,
his popularity swells
as each banker
locks up his stocks
and his daughters.

Harriet Harman seethes,
remembers her student days
when she too felt
a little more remorse and understanding
for the poorest and downtrodden.

Then shakes away those memories
of spliffs and Trotsky and *The Second Sex*,
sends out a list of suspicious names
on the hard left.

Liz Kendall breathes fire
from her East Midlands ivory tower,
calls the people of Leicester
to promise to vote for her,
holding their council tax rates in one hand
and a crossbow in the other.

Smiling Yvette Cooper,
blank-faced and glazed over,
vows to get down off that fence
one side or another
just as soon as someone
elects her as leader.

Andy Burnham's clutching at straws,
searching Corbyn's floor
for anything we might recognise
as radical.

Behind closed doors
they weep uncontrollably
at the control they're rapidly losing
over their centre-left Labour party,
rueing the day they ever gave
this much power to the electorate,
warning of decades in opposition,
raising the ghost of Michael Foot.

Crying and lying,
stomping and trying
to turn the head of the voter
away from this Mumsnet wooer,
this white-haired, soft-eyed
night bus rider,
slimmed-down Bernard Cribbins,
caped crusader,
revolutionary anti-tie wearer
fighting for the right to wear plaid
and a corduroy cardie.
He's calm and he's cool,
takes no shit
from Krishnan Guru-Murthy,
he's hot stuff
and old stuff,
sixty-six going on sexy.
He's strawberries,
oysters,
Careless Whisper,
a kaftan,
a flat cap,
and he's never been
more hated by Labour.

Because despite telling us
they are the party of the left wing,
Corbyn actually means it.
That's why there's just no place
for him.

NUMBER 81

The walls are thudding
like my least favourite band through mud.
This is like being stuck in the dance tent
at Glastonbury 2016
when it had rained for four days solidly
and I'd had cystitis since we'd got there
so I'd just had the one green tea
all evening,
except on top of the thudding
is their
I don't give a fuck
laughing.

And they don't
give any fucks
because they're so young
they believe the world
owes them something.
Every time we've been round
to ask them to turn it down
they tell us
why should they have to
change anything about themselves
just because they live next door
to these two idiots?

My dentist gave me a mouth guard
to wear at night
because stress is making me grind my teeth.
The stress of wearing this thing
that makes me look like a boxer
on top of their thudding laughter
is going to see me turn my teeth to dust.

And I hate them.
And the bed is moving
inch by inch across the floor.

We've been round
six times since Tuesday
and the one with so much lip liner
she looks like a *Star Wars* villain
always answers.
She's always wearing
some sort of lacy negligée.
I want to say,
You are a student.
Where are your worn-down trackies
and Subway-stained T-shirt?
What woman
who isn't Holly Golightly
has any use
for this sort of see-through
undergarment?

But I don't.

Because I tried that approach
last week,
so now I'm just sobbing in my slippers
in the street
and it may as well be raining
for how pathetic this is.

Three days ago
I promised myself
she would not reduce me to this,
but she has,
because she's won.
I don't care.
I just need some sleep.

I tell her,
I'm in a school tomorrow.
I'm up at six tomorrow.
I'm doing a twelve-hour day tomorrow.

15

Except tomorrow is today
and the sun's coming up.
She's laughing at my pleading,
slams the door in my face.

We take back to our bed,
holding hands across the mattress
like the last survivors on a sinking ship.
He says,
Maybe we should call the police?
but we tried that
twice.
They don't come.
They just tell us that
due to budget cuts
there are only ever two officers
on duty on any one day.

I hate you, Theresa May.

You try living in this
two-up
two-down
terrace
where there is no escape
from *Blurred Lines*
for a third time.

I say,
Let's try and do some yoga breathing,
but on the third exhalation
another speaker kicks in.

He says,
We are intelligent adults;
we just need to stay strong,
but she's

just
so
young.

The first time we chanced a complaint,
she scoffed at our half-nine
bedtime routine,
but when you're eighteen
ten Jägerbombs
and an hour's sleep
is a bloody luxury,
then ten years creep by
and you're happy with
a small wine and
I'll just stay up to watch the headlines.

So I wish
this liplined girl child
the worst night
since she downed her first
Smirnoff Ice.

I wish her empty dance floors.
I wish her lights as bright
as a Topshop changing room;
you can see every make-up mistake.
Is that a grey?

(I like grey hair.
I have a lot of my own.
It makes me feel like Rogue from *X-Men*.
But I know she won't;
she will care.
I want her to care.
I want her to care
as much as I do at 6am
when the alarm's just gone off
and I've been asleep since 5.45.)

I wish her stale wine.
I wish her watered-down pints.
I wish her *Agadoo* played six times.
I wish her her drunk mum appearing in the same club, out for
    her book group's bi-monthly social.
I wish her tired friends who want to be home by ten when she
    spent four hours getting ready for this long-anticipated
    freshers' event.
I wish her a crying best mate who just bumped into her ex.
I wish her closed pubs and smudged mascara.
I wish her her skirt tucked into her knickers with friends too
    callous to tell her
so it just stays that way for hours
and they're her worst pants,
bought in Year 9
by her nan
from a sale in BHS,
the ones saved for the days
when the washing machine's broken
and a state of emergency has been called.
They're yellowed
and baggy
with long-snapped elastic.
They used to have a pattern of dogs on
but after five years of washes the pattern's long gone;
now they're just covered in questionable
faded brown spots.

I hate her.

As much as she hates me.

After telling her I was a teacher
because I had hoped it would make her take me more
seriously,
I hope this poem gets back to her.
I just want
some fucking
sleep.

RESTART

Written for students at Beaumont Leys School, Leicester

My mum was a teacher,
my sister a five-year-ahead success.
I had the odds stacked in my favour.
No one was going to let
me do any less
than my absolute best in any
exam, coursework or revision test.

At thirteen
I was crawling out of every lesson
on my belly
under desks,
spending more and more hours
in behaviour support
under the teacher's frown.
Every time my mum was called in
to explain why I was messing around
or doing something badly
or doing something wrong
or just not doing anything at all
again
I sank lower in my chair
outside the head's office.
I lowered my glare.
I expected her to be
mad and angry.
She never was,
not really.
Just sad and scared,
until one day
she said,
You don't understand.
If you mess this up
through laziness
and taking the mick

they won't let you back again.
If you open the envelope
and don't like what you see on the page
there is no restart button.
There is no
'whoops, messed that up royally,
I'll go back to Year 7 and have another go'.
They will let you go into adulthood
with a shrug
and a 'just make the best of it'.

It doesn't need to be like that.

Summon all the forethought you have
to see a life
where you hold every skill you possess
close to your chest,
even the boring ones
you're convinced you will never use,
because there are still times
I'm embarrassed
my accountant
has to do my long division for me.
He finishes each sum
with a smile and flourish.
Don't worry.
Most women aren't good at maths.

Even if that were true,
I could have been.

I'm embarrassed
that there are girls around the world
risking bullets, blood,
kidnap, torture,
being strung up in the street
just to learn,

when I spent three years
backchatting my French teacher
with grammatically incorrect
Spanish swear words

instead of thinking
that here and now
was this window of opportunity.

In every Year 11 assembly
we had a teacher
who told us repeatedly
that we were made of stardust,
so how could we just waste
all of that positive energy?
His whitewash
broad-brush
statements made me cringe,
but ten years on
I still see time like a tide coming in.

You feel like you've got all this time
to get everything done.
You don't hear the tide
sniggering up to your ankles
until you're swimming
in all those things
you said you'd do next week.

I admit
there are things
I'm not designed to understand.
Selfies and fashion magazines
go hand in hand
at the top of the list,
but the number-one thing
that makes my skin itch
with irritation

is smooth-faced celebrities
who are made famous for playing thick.

Who go on panel shows
to stare down the lens of a camera
in feigned bafflement
because having no answers
or imagination
is their thing,
who giggle
in open-mouthed amusement
that they have no idea
where Germany is
or what an aubergine looks like
or *what is their opinion*
of the kidnapping of hundreds of girls
by Boko Haram
who just wanted to go to school?

Laugh it off,
go back to plugging
your next ghostwritten book.

There are things I don't know.
They are plentiful.

I always struggled to remember
anything to do with the periodic table.
It took real effort
to memorise it for my GCSE.
I panic at map reading,
lie about the fact
that I use a satnav
to make it to most places.
I was once asked to do an interview
for the *New Statesman*,
turned it down

because I was scared I'd look stupid.
I watch *University Challenge*
and don't even understand the questions.
Despite a love of cake
and Mary Berry,
I cannot bake.
I just burn it.

I am embarrassed by these things
and I'm trying to be better.

Why would you not want
to be the most interesting person
in every room you're in?

Wear your intelligence
next to each book you've read
like diamonds on a necklace
or chinks in a four-figure-cost
wristwatch
that glints with each
practised flick of the wrist.

Have each and every answer
at the ready,
be steady in your delivery,
never be dumbfounded
by a question you weren't expecting.

On the days
when you are one week away
from something very important,
you've revised until you're reciting
French verbs in your sleep,
skimmed and scanned every fact sheet,
filled your bathroom walls up
with pages of maths equations

to go over again
when you're brushing your teeth,
still you feel like the failure
you fear you'll be.
With a stone in your tummy,
frustration in your fists,
when your brain feels
like an oversaturated sieve,
day-to-day conversations
make you tear up.
Your mate's acting tough,
he won't speak to you
because you won't go out tonight,
he's as pent-up,
has had enough of this pressure,
the weight on his back as you.

Hold your nerve,
hold your tongue,
find the breath in your belly,
hold on to the feeling
of having done your best,
not wanting to press
the restart button.

FRIDAY NIGHT

My stomach fills
with the feeling of a weekend
not spent worrying about work and money
but sipping pints,
hearing stories of other people's
hard-worked days.
We laugh at how boring we've become
when ten minutes are spent talking
about broadband providers
and pension schemes.
We leave the pub
with the promise
of a takeaway and board games.

Amongst the night-fuelled voices
he says,
A bomb's gone off in Paris,
and I almost miss it.

Isn't Twitter always filled
with the violence of countries
we were just lucky enough
not to have been born in?
Through the barrage
of opinions and information
we cherry-pick the ones
that move us into action.

I get myself distracted,
let this news pass me by,
put on music,
find the corkscrew,
laugh at a joke told twice
because the first time
nobody noticed.

Friday nights

are made for this,
wine and chat,
jokes and gossip,
for your favourite film,
your comfiest pyjamas,
the most expensive ready meal,
watching crap telly
with your parents,
trying that new sushi place,
spilling beer on your dress
and not caring,
for being a teenager
wearing a brand new pair
of Converse trainers
to a rock gig
because you saved up for weeks
to buy a ticket.
For first dates,
fiftieth dates,
standing in the street
with your best mate
laughing so hard
neither of you can speak,
your mascara's running streams
down your cheeks,
what makes it all the funnier
is that neither of you
can remember what was so funny
in the first place.
For holding hands across a table,
going to a football match,
going to the theatre,
taking selfies in celebration
of the fact
this is the first time
since the baby was born
that you've actually made it out the house together.

Friday nights
are made for laughter,
the rise before the beat drops,
the bridge before the chorus,
the opening bars of your favourite song,
the audience knowing every word
in time,
flawless.

Nobody told those kids
at that gig
they were going to war.

They were dressed up,
hyped up, excited
with their mates.
When the first gunshot
went off,
I bet some of them had their
arms around strangers.

Music doesn't see the gaps between people;
it just tells you
to throw off your insecurities
and enjoy it.

Nobody has the right
to say that's wrong,
to decide who lives and dies,
even when Cameron's
bragging about dropping bombs.
I'm with Corbyn on this one.
That hate breeds hate,
death breeds death.
Friday nights are sacred.

To have a few hours

out of the working week
to not feel scared
or sad
or worried.
To put an arm around a shoulder,
take a hand,
look into the face
of someone you love and say,
*Shall we get a drink
and have a dance?*

HELD BACK BY NICKY MORGAN

Post-show,
the lights have come up,
empty plastic wine glasses
litter the floor,
I'm in the bar next door
trying to calm down,
rein the adrenaline in,
go through the couple of mistakes I made,
see how they match up to yesterday,
put steps in place
to rectify them for tomorrow night.

He sidles up to me with a grin.

Is this your hobby or something?

It's my job.

No way, he says.
You get paid for this?
This is how you make a living?
There are kids starving in the world
and whilst we pay our taxes
you ponce about on stage?

His argument is nonsensical
and it's flawed.
It's not like
I haven't heard it before,
but this time
it seems to hurt harder,
sting faster,
because now Nicky Morgan
has added fuel to the fire
of their argument
that this isn't a real job.
I walk away,

swallow my reply,
not thinking about
the three hours
I spent rehearsing that afternoon,
the ninety-minute tech run-through this evening,
the four trips to the toilet
before the lights came down
because I thought I might be sick.
The twice-weekly meet-ups
in rehearsal rooms,
the days and evenings
with blank pages and frustration,
the ten minutes stolen
in a school car park
trying to get a piece finished for a deadline,
every street run down
to make the last train in time,
the nights out ended early
and the friends cancelled on
to finish work that couldn't wait,
every funding application scrawled across
the thank you, but unfortunately… replies.
The clock at midnight
when we've still not got something
we can agree is right,
the bags under our eyes
when I say,
Let's just go through this one more time,
the days disappeared into nights
trying to learn it
line for line,

all of that

for Nicky Morgan to tell me
that the choices I have made
will hold me back
for the rest of my life.

Promote science,
please do,
and maths and technology and engineering,
they're important
and have their own issues,
but in the rare position you hold
where young people
might actually listen to you,
don't write off great swathes
of something so crucial
to our day-to-day.

Don't insult the teachers
who, alongside the facts and the figures,
teach the stories and the sounds and the pictures
and the message
Do something you love and work hard at it,
whatever it is.

Don't make some broad-brush statement
about arts and humanities
limiting somebody's life choices.

You're the mother of the girl at my school
who said,
Don't go to university
and study creative writing.
No one makes a living
from being a writer.
You'll end up
in some dead-end job
wishing you'd done maths.
So she did maths,
was good at it,
became an accountant.
I saw her on a train
last Tuesday;

she said she earns
sixty grand a year,
wakes up most days
fighting the urge to hate herself.

You're my old boss who said,
Well, it's a nice hobby, isn't it,
but is that really how you want to
spend your spare time,
getting up at five just to write?
Anyway,
the bags under your eyes
are affecting productivity.

You make it sound like something dirty,
to be done in garages and lofts,
the occasional
run-down
funding-starved library,
not something
that lets us talk
down the generations
and back through history.

From the fingerprint-moulded
shapes on the walls of caves
to plays that brought culture to the day-to-day
peasant and drunkard
in the theatre pit,
every fear- and anger-fuelled war poet
from 'Charge of the Light Brigade'
to Siegfried Sassoon
(how else would we have taught
World War One
in the days before YouTube?),
the teenage girl
terrified in a secret attic room,

every child
who learnt empathy
from a book
that teaches strength and courage
against the worst of enemies,
the poem that attacks
the stuck-up out-of-touch politician,
the pints raised
in recognition
of the stories told
by folk musicians,
the boy wrapped up in autism
who struggles to communicate through emotion
but can tell you how he feels
with colour and sound
or the refugee
too scared to speak
who finds words on the lips
of hip-hop artists,
begins writing her own lyrics,
discovers what her art is.

Don't belittle this.

By all means
stand at your lectern, spout the opinions
you think will win you votes
like they all do,
but don't scaremonger,
don't guilt-trip,
don't tell the fourteen-year-old
with a form to fill in
if you love what you do
there is ever any reason

to stop doing it.

NATIONAL AVERAGE

From the moment they take
their first breath
they're marked in line
with the baby next to them
for weight and height
and the day they take their first steps
against their age and class
and social standing
so when they're toddling in line
with the baby next to them
on the first day of reception
they are ready to be graded,
tried and tested,
marked in line
with the national average,
where every child
must stand above
the national average,
because where's progress
unless based on a handful
of flimsy statistics?

School halls are crammed
with podgy-limbed toddlers
wondering who took their
sandpits away,
replaced them
with a paper and pen
they are yet to learn
how to hold.

Later, when they're told
their score,
their mark,
their grade
for their baseline assessment,
they're learning

their first lesson
in how to deal with consequences
of actions
they weren't even aware of making.

Now we know
that you are John,
your mum took you to the theatre
from the age of two,
played you Mozart
while you were still in the womb,
before you even had the consciousness
to understand this would
stand you in good stead
for this day.

You are Hayley,
whose house was a little more complicated,
never taken to the theatre
to see the adaptation
of *Dogs Don't Do Ballet*,
whose parents
scrabbled down the sofa
for pennies,
then decided
whether to spend them
on heating or eating,
given it was now coming up to
the third of January.

Done and dusted.
Thank God we managed
to get that sorted.

Now carry that score card
with you
until the next time
you're tested.

In the meantime
they're told to
express themselves
in active voices
using conjunctive adverbs,
subordinate clauses,
learn history
chronologically,
which means it's
intensely boring
as soon as you
get past the dinosaurs.

Here comes another round
of tests and assessments.
This time they're just old enough
to hold on to the idea
that if they don't do well enough
they're probably
just not good enough.

At least not as good as that
golden pie in the sky
called the national average,
ever unreachable
except for the most privileged.

In Year 6
we were still picking up bugs
and wetting our knickers
from too much giggling.
Now I stand in primary school corridors
lined with signs
saying,
Shh, exam in progress.

Like the ones you see

during your GCSEs,
your A-levels
and the final year
of your degree.

These are scraped-knee children
with the remnants
of dinner round their faces
swapping football stickers
in the queue for the
exam papers.

Even the ones
awarded more time,
the slow readers,
the ones with special needs
and statements
spend it
watery-eyed
in empty classrooms,
looking pleadingly
from their teachers
to the sunshine outside,
remembering a time
when just painting
a picture of your goldfish
was enough to get you
a *well done.*

At least they have their
post-test party
to look forward to,
popcorn,
pizza,
Ice Age 2
on the big projector,
where everyone in the room

can feel like
they're all in this together,
remember
they are eleven years old.

Except Nicky Morgan
called ahead
to say these frivolities
are to be cancelled
from today
because there is no space
in the curriculum
for a whole-class flash mob
of *Gangnam Style*
or for Henry Jones,
for whom
the national average
is but a wondrous dream,
to sing his own rendition
of *Let It Go*.

No,
the only glimmer of hope
is one rogue marker
with whom all teachers
are standing up
like Spartacus.

Little chinks
in the armour
like the Schools Minister
unable to correctly
answer a question
from the very test he
so protectively
crows over.

Surely it's not meant to be
such a damn hard slog?
It's meant to be
numbers, words,
science experiments,
playing, painting,
chanting the wives
of Henry VIII,
red puffed faces
from scorch-hot
sports days,
celebrating the achievements
of each individual,
whether that's
fractions,
dancing,
knowing all the songs from *The Jungle Book*.

It's not meant to be
tests,
stress,
impossible questions.
Let them enjoy a time
when school is supposed to be
fun with your mates,
working out what you're good at,
not always being the best.
When you don't know, well,
a guess is as good as being correct.

Just let them get on with it.
Don't brand them
with labels and marks
that do nothing but
make them feel thick.
Remember they're children,
so let kids be kids,
not some national average
statistic.

INVISIBLE

She says she does not see them
even though her eyes are open,
but they do not gather
at the door of her North London town house,
nor in the gardens of her brother's Hampshire estate,
neither do they appear
where the beach meets the sea
at her coastal home.
She is looking but finds their existence hard to believe.

Everyone seems to be doing well for themselves these days,
don't they?
Unemployment down,
FTSE 100 up,
people still out shopping in
Joules, Ted Baker and M&S.

She holds her hands out like they span the country,
asks me to pinpoint the poor
I am always banging on about.

But it is dinner time
and aged twenty-eight I have learnt when my mum
would rather I stopped talking, digging,
winding this woman next to her up.

The previous week
I am at our local Labour party meeting.
We meet in the smallest room
in a neighbourhood centre.
At the beginning everyone chips in
for the cost of the room hire.
The man at the front
has been invited to speak to us
about Universal Credit.
No, he does not mind
they spelt his name incorrectly on the agenda.

He is non-partisan,
he says three times.
He cannot stress that enough.
He is not here to campaign,
just here to give the information we requested.
He's worked in the benefit office for fifteen years,
grew up under Thatcher as a kid,
but those days were nothing compared to this;
at least she didn't make a secret of it,
didn't speak through awkward stooped false smiles
and proclaim
the six-week wait is for the benefit of all,
and then with an entirely straight face he says,

Universal Credit is designed to kill off the poor.

A woman in a wheelchair at the back agrees,
describes these new systems as a death sentence,
DSA, ESA, PIP.
Her and her friends have a support group
to help each other through this.
They've lost three this year.
It is February.

Three strikes and you're down.
The first two meetings
are always in towns you have never heard of,
miles away,
Monday mornings,
9am.
If you don't make it
you have one chance left.
In the building
next to the multistorey car park.
Interviews are held on the top floor.
If you cannot take the stairs
there is a lift,

except they are not insured for wheelchair users
in case of fire,
so with no prior warning
you are taxied to the next city over.
If you have plans
or the school run
or just don't want to go to Nottingham,
you are handed a flyer
for the local food bank.

The woman shrugs.
The man at the front
says this American company
have not been tasked with helping anybody.
Nobody gets a kindness bonus.
Their aim is to get you off their books
by any means necessary.
They earn commission
by being callous, hard and sneaky.

I do two hours in that food bank
every other Tuesday.
Demand has risen by 30%.
We pack a box every 2.7 minutes
for the guy who sleeps behind Aldi
and eats out the skip,
for the retired nurse who hands
over her voucher,
shellshocked, unblinking.

We hand out phones and tablets
to complete Universal Credit applications.
Brian is eighty,
has no internet access,
and when he went to the library he's relied on for years
there was a *closed* sign on the door.

The woman next to him
was asked to pay back
to the benefit office
a £1,000 overspend,
and when she said she didn't have that money to hand
they slapped her with a year's sanction
to think about what she'd done.
She asks if we have any nappies for her baby of nine months.
Could we throw in a few extra tins?
It's not official, but she's had a friend and her kids
on her sofa the past three weeks.

Her friend's a primary school teacher
with six weeks' holiday and a pension.
When the private landlord upped the rent
for all his tenants
in fear of losing out to Universal Credit
and the gas bill increased just as fast as the cost of living,
she couldn't keep hold of the house or the cat.
Now she sofa-surfs
with three under-tens.
It's been three months.
No one at work suspects,
but she's running out of friends
and they're running out of patience
and the council housing waiting list
is six months at best.
Her starting salary won't cover the cost of a deposit
and two months' advance rent,
so she shuffles the kids past beggars
and sleeping bags in doorways,
hoping that one day
she might get some of that performance-related pay
people keep telling her about.

Back around the dinner table,
we are at the tail end of a bank holiday weekend,

my mum is giving me daggers
but, fuelled with the confidence
of half a bottle of red,
I ask this woman opposite me,
holding her hands out like they span the country,

How has it come to this?

That the people at the top have pulled the ladder
so far up
they've forgotten the people at the bottom even exist?

That gap has been filled with
fear,
Farage,
Katie Hopkins,
tabloid rhetoric.

Meanwhile
bankers,
MPS,
CEOs,
prime ministers,
government departments,
lords and boards,
the highest-earning second home earners

say they just don't see it,

too distracted by headlines
pointing over the water
to his finger hovering over the button
like a bored judge at a singing contest.
Never mind your empty cupboards,
your failing health service;
watch him.

What will he do next?

Blow the whole world to bits,
then you'll feel like an idiot
for moaning about your six-week wait
and your Universal Credit.

EXCUSE ME, MR CORBYN, THERESA'S ON THE PHONE

April 2017

Organic marrow in one hand,
a thirst for social justice in the other,
he smooths down the breast of his cardigan,
excuses himself from the meeting of UK cheese makers
and rises.

AS A NEW MEMBER OF THE LABOUR PARTY YOU ARRIVE AT THE SPECIFIED ADDRESS CLUTCHING A BOTTLE OF CAB SAV

Welcome!
Come on in;
door's always open
(apart from that brief period
when Harriet Harman began ejecting members
she felt were on the hard left,
but we've spoken to her about that).

All in all
we're a broad church.
Leave your coat on the bed.

Excuse the music.

You'll see we've assigned you the main hall.
Note the hammer and sickle bunting.

In the side room,
dancing ironically to noughties indie hits,
the centrist city workers
(don't say bank,
say financial sector),
a lot of them old student union officers
still with a thirst for democracy,
still here by the skin of their teeth,
too sane for the Lib Dems,
too state-schooled for the Tories.

Don't miss the parents' silent disco at ten,
Tony on the decks
playing D:Ream
over and over again,

staring into the middle distance,
don't mention Iraq,
don't mention Iraq,
don't mention Iraq,
anything to stop them
remembering the disappointment,
keep them pointing at Corbyn
chanting the word
UNELECTABLE
at their
all of a sudden
activist kids.

We've set aside the room
with the en suite
for the Labour students,
ready for their
2am legal high trips.

Out fighting topless in the garden,
the trade unionists.
Someone said
maybe they didn't need another meeting
to discuss the future of the movement.

Down here in the kitchen
the interns who work for the party,
live in South London
but flown into marginal seats.
We're making an effort
to keep them away
from all the local councillors
they've made feel inadequate.
Don't worry, guys,
more salmon roulade on its way.

I'll leave you to grab a drink.
Just careful in the corridors
lined with older members
wearing their 1965 membership cards
as name badges,
playing Education Secretary Top Trumps
and challenging each other
to remember the finer points of
the 1998 Waste Minimisation Act.

WHAT WILL SURVIVE OF US

He was here with my sister
the day my granddad died,
digging up parsnips for dinner,
late eighties, mobileless,
Mum screaming over the fence.

Then me in rolled-up dungarees
being generally unhelpful with a watering can
before teenage angst and furious sighs
every time I caught sight of him.

Now between hospital trips,
scans, tests, ECGs,
we pile over for a glimpse
of his weekend retreat,
seedlings, makeshift compost heap,
scarecrows from general election posters,
wood plank walkways,
a bottle of BrewDog,
the wind-up radio
left from a time
before podcasts
on Bluetooth headphones.

Every third person here's on warfarin.
He'll be in good company.
They nod and wander over
to trade stories
of potatoes, heart valves,
cutting down,
confirming the date
of the next
seed swap,
cider press,
bonfire day,
what morning is the leaf man coming?

TWENTY-THREE WAYS OF LOOKING AT MY EXCEPTION TO THE RULE

I have never seen anyone
commit to dancing to a live band
on such a serious level.

You have unironically worn your
Andrew WK
Party Hard T-shirt
to every one of my niece and nephew's
birthday parties.

Your bloody frustrating optimism.

The night you turned up
at my sister's house at 10pm
after four pints in the pub
with a Tupperware box
to remove a dead mouse
from her saucepan cupboard.

The time you fixed a tent pole
on the side of a hill
in a thunderstorm
at a drum 'n' bass festival
neither of us wanted to be at.

You smile at dogs.
Not at their owners.

You always find the good in people,
even when they don't deserve it.

Your musical knowledge.
Up to and including
the night we went to a folk club
in Robin Hood's Bay,
surrounded by a Great Dane

and six men in their eighties
all singing songs in Gaelic.
You were heralded
as a hero for singing along
the loudest,
word perfect.

How good you are.

Your commitment to other people's welfare
which sits in correlation
to how much of a stranger they are to you.

Like the night Scott lost his wellies
in the mud at Glastonbury
and had to stand barefoot
waiting for you to help
every passing person
over two feet of particularly
slippy puddle
for twenty-five minutes
before you remembered he was still there,
still in bare feet.

You can only do one thing at a time,
but your commitment to that thing
exceeds all rational explanation:
brewing beer,
playing the guitar,
the preparation required for a six-hour game of *Eldritch Horror*.

Your utmost honesty,
apart from when you've eaten something
you've later discovered was mine
out the fridge.

That the phrase *organisational skills*
sends you into a blind panic.

That you will answer the phone to me
twenty foot off the ground, installing a CCTV system
on the third floor of a tower block
from the top of a cherry picker,
and still say no, you're not busy.

I have lost count of the number of bands you are in.
I think you have as well.

That we can walk into a bookshop
anywhere in the world
and I can guarantee you will walk out
carrying a tome on ancient mythology or Norse gods.

The time I got you up at 6am
for an education cuts protest
you had only agreed to come on to humour me,
but by midday
you had acquired a whistle, were holding the banner
and wouldn't stop calling me *comrade*.

My twenty-sixth birthday,
when you mixed up Thomas Hardy
with the Brontës
but only realised when we were in standstill traffic
on the drive down to Dorchester.

When we'd been together a month
I went on holiday
and you spent every evening I was away
finishing my decorating
because you knew I'd never get round
to painting behind the toilet.

On our first date
I invited you to a poetry slam
in a shady pub

I was performing at
to an audience of just one.
You spent the entire evening sat alone,
drinking Coke
because you'd driven straight from work,
and were inexplicably wearing a T-shirt
that said LOCKSMITH on the front.

I still hadn't thought of asking
what it was you did for a living,
too keen to make sure you thought I was interesting,
and still now,
on evenings when I have talked at you for two hours
on a varying range of themes,
my inexhaustible stream of consciousness,
I am so pleased
you're still listening.

PORTALOO QUEUE

A man with bin bags tied to his feet
mops condom wrappers and used tampons into the mud
as a woman in a sequinned Barbour jacket
tells us she drank for free in the bar last night
because she's mates with Tracy Barlow off *Coronation Street*.

BALFOUR ROAD

Two miles along the coast,
past the castle, Timeball Tower, rotting boats,
all my dad's ghosts,
smell of coal fire
could be something my memory's created
like the anxiety that's been dogging me for days.

The money hasn't flowed this far up,
the Dover Road pocked with kebab houses and betting shops,
a breaker against the wine bars and micro-breweries.

I don't know what she'd make of it,
Farrow & Ball,
wood-burning stoves
with her coal-burnt carpet round the fireplace,
pantry,
single glazing,
seventies kitchen
that matched the colour of the teacups,
cabbage green,
my aunt with a motorbike in the back garden,
my dad's silence,
me on the Bakelite telephone telling Mum
about swimming in the Deal sea
in February.

Me and my sister in dolls' house
side-by-side pastel pink beds,
my dad awake next door
in the bed he was born in,
lying on top of all her unblinking portraits
she stored underneath.

I do love it when you come to visit.

Google Maps says one more minute.
On the corner a woman in a green jumper
hunched over, pruning.

I walk the street to the end with the garage
where she fell and hit her head.
I was sick in the car.
Dad had to call an ambulance.

I walk back to the corner,
woman in the green jumper.
A man dressed as a pound sign
gets out of a Land Rover,
goes into the house
where hers used to be.

THANK GOD

The day gone,
now just *Gogglebox*,
mid-range wine,
bed socks,
still early enough
for the doorbell to ring
with takeaway.
Next door the neighbours
get ready to go clubbing
and how relieved we are
that that's no longer us.

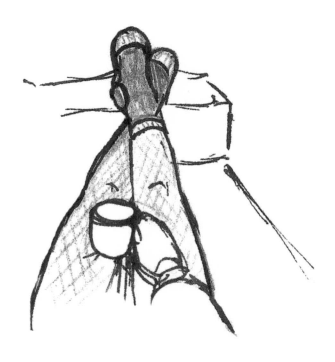

CHECK

A map of all the light switches in the house
plug sockets
fire sources
when did we last test the smoke alarms?
carbon monoxide detectors
open windows
all the ways an intruder could kill the dog
unlocked doors
gas hobs
grill
are the taps off?
flooding
the dog drowns
fire bomb through the letter box
is the door locked?
laptop spontaneously combusts
because I didn't turn it off
dog flap
cat burglar
back gate
out house
warm enough?
(for the dog)
too cold
burst pipes
house flooded
drowned dog
did I leave my straighteners on?
did I leave my straighteners on?
did I leave my straighteners on?
front door shut
front door locked
are you sure?
I'll just go back and

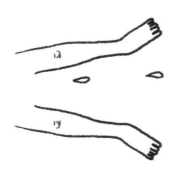

HIGH ART

Me and Alison went to see it
after all the hype it had got on Twitter,
protest art meets physical theatre.
Alison had a spare ticket
and at Glastonbury that summer
I'd heard one of Pussy Riot speaking about it,
which meant I immediately ticked

every
white,
middle-class
and artsy
box of its demographic.

I don't know what I expected.

I guess I was hoping for fury,
to feel the energy that drives protests forward,
red flags,
chants
barricades,
all the feelings I have for Corbyn,

a tongue-in-cheek jibe
at the division of the left
or at least a reinforcement
of my own frustrated echo chamber,

but what we got
was a stage of naked men
setting things on fire
with no explanation.
It may have been a metaphor.
I don't know.
I was too busy
making a mental risk assessment.
An actor was stabbed in the leg,
then hung up from the lighting rig.
He then proceeded to piss
on the rest of the cast below.

After the piss
came the spit,
the blood,
the vomit.
It was real.

You could smell it.

Then torture,
then screaming,
then beating,
all set to a background of strobe lights
and sweating
and swearing
and drowning

followed by an absurd Q&A
where no one could think of a single question,
and all of this went on
with not one hint of an interval
for 120 minutes.

We were meant to be shocked,
which I was
to start off with,
but after a fifteen-minute silent fight scene
all done in mime
the impact wore off.

Until boredom saw me counting the seats,
eyes glazed,
trying to recreate that episode of *Supervet*
I was missing.

When it finally ended
the actors appeared,
nonchalant,
clothed,
mainstream,
waving.

The tallest,
now let down from the lighting rig,
reminded us that
this show had been inspiring.
He said he was giving us permission
to go create change in our own communities.

The audience loved this.
The applause was cacophonous
until he was shouting over the rapture
a reminder

that we should not stand for oppression,
we should not stand for
budget cuts,
the bedroom tax,
payday loans,
zero-hour contracts,
we should not stand for
the rich getting richer
while the poor use food banks.

Like he was Ken Loach
at the BAFTAs
the audience put down their glasses of shiraz
for a standing ovation
up on their feet
from seats that cost them
twenty-three quid a ticket.

They left with renewed activism,
ready to fight
at weekends and on bank holidays
from Twitter and on the commute,
no more Starbucks,

no more Amazon,
we'll be more intelligent
about where we get our news.

In a review the next day
the *Independent* said this was
a five-star example of art house theatre
through the eyes of Russian postmodernism.

Good.
We'll just keep
retweeting
that until the government has fallen.

In the meantime
the *Daily Mail* will continue
to fill its front pages
with hate speech,
make a mockery of the EU-loving liberal elite.

The *Guardian* will revel in their favourite headline
that protest art is dead,
no more Billy,

no more Sex Pistols,
no more Angry Young Men.

Instead
it exists in fifty-foot glass buildings
where the tickets cost
the same as the weekly shop.

Even if you make it to your seat
you need a PhD in art history
for it to make any sense.

Show me the link between
a naked man in a motorbike helmet
and a better-funded NHS
or a stage full of bodily fluids
and a solution to the refugee crisis,

but when fascism is
holding hands
with our Prime Minister
and *send them back* Theresa
looks positively liberal but terrified

in comparison with this guy
and what's real but long-winded
is sidelined
by what's exciting and concise,
looks nice in 140 characters,
turns out to be a pack of lies,

then don't we need protest art that's relevant,
that speaks to the many and not the few?

That's
subsidised,
energising,
funny,
thrilling,
dirty,
dark,
tragic
and taboo?

That's taken out of stuffy spaces,
put in places it can be discovered,

in parks, pubs, community centres,
open-mics,
on the telly,
on the BBC,
in living rooms,
at folk nights,
on the internet,
on Instagram,
in YouTube clips,
not just under stage lights?

If you're going to tell me about oppression,
go ahead,
have a man pissing on himself from the lighting rig,
but also show me
food parcels,
homelessness,
the unravelling of a safety net,
job centres,
benefit offices,
the collapse of public services,
gay rights,
the right to strike,

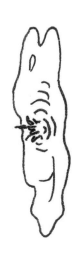

ever-expanding twelve-week waiting lists,
and on the darkest, most frustrating days
don't let the answers exist
in places created by those who can afford a ticket.

Let them exist not just in theatres
but in the hearts and eyes of normal folk,
so that in centuries to come
we'll look back on this and say
that protest art wasn't dead;
it was protest art that won.

PORT ISAAC

Martin Clunes not in.
Heard he does all his scenes in a week,
leaves the others to fill in the rest.
Still, we saw the chemist in a neck brace.
Maybe we could leak that on Twitter,
the big *Doc Martin* neck brace spoiler,
sell it to *Heat* magazine.
It might cover the cost
of this prawn sandwich.

SNOOPERS' CHARTER

I won't track this
third slice of lemon cheesecake
in any of my seven calorie-counting apps
just in case.
I like to give a good impression of myself.

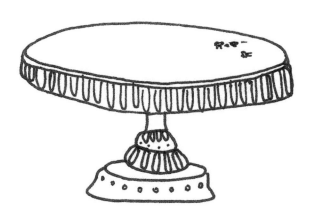

CHINESE WHISPERS

It's in every woman you tell it to
and if not her then her sister,
blink and you miss it,
in strip-lit council flat kitchens,
early-hour terraced houses,
uni halls,
care homes,
we take out the guilt from below the gut,
back of the head,
hold it up next to all the times it got too much,
make comparisons with hers.

Then finish the bottle,
wash up the teacup,
stub out the cigarette butt,
quietly hug,
apologise for saying too much, again,
go back to our jobs
in banks and schools and supermarket checkouts,
wash the kids,
feed the dog.

Thumb silent likes
on sympathetic headlines,
Kesha,
Taylor Swift,
the Rochdale girls.
Then phone away,
we get on the bus,
order a pint,
open the book where we left it,

and you don't notice us
catch each other's eyes.

FROM THOSE OPENING TRUMPETS

I will row with you
long past last orders
loud enough for the rest of the pub
to think that we are married
and you've had an affair
when you say you don't agree
that parallels can be drawn
between *Coronation Street*
and the works of Shakespeare.

BALLAD OF THE UNEMPLOYED
ARTS GRADUATE

Mum always thought I'd get a job with the Labour party,
write a novel in the evenings,
except I was twenty-one
and had just been to a Kate Tempest gig,
so two weeks before graduation
I told her I had decided to become a poet.

It was all going to be very exciting
in my garret,
cigarettes and notebooks,
tortured artist.
Think Nemo in *Bleak House*
with more Leonard Cohen.

I'd get a cat,
have a string of lovers,
beat back the literati from the front door
just as soon as I was discovered by the *Guardian*.

Age thirty,
I have a husband,
a dog,
and every so often
appear in the *Leicester Mercury*.
The novelty of telling my partner's parents' friends
I'm a *writer* for a living
has worn off.
Now I just crumble into vague
and babbling embarrassment.
If I can't face it
and will never see them again
I say I'm an English teacher
for fear they'll ask,
Have you written anything we would have heard of?

Not unless you have a good memory for vintage YouTube
    videos.

Even TS Eliot kept his job in the bank,
didn't wander blindly
with swaggering enthusiasm
into the abyss.

How I despise all those quiet girls I went to school with
whose mothers always said they couldn't come swimming
because they had too much homework to do,
whose profile pictures now show them
swimming in the Bahamas
with two privately educated daughters
they can afford to raise,
not camping in a field with their parents
who they themselves were hoping
retirement would bring freedom from weekends away
with their permanently broke and scruffy youngest.

In response to news of my future career path
my mum asked me why I felt
more people didn't become
full-time freelance poets.
Because they're boring.
They've probably never thought about it.
Maybe they just know they'd be rubbish?

Because, Mum,
some people are born to be accountants
and some of us are born to be artists.

This too was my response
when, drinking in the student union,
speccy men would make fun
of my Mickey Mouse degree.
Now they're working in
banking,
oil,
managing wind farms off the coast of France.

I go round to my mum's house once a week
to see what she's got going off in her fridge
that I can eat.

I still dress like a teenager
and call it fashion
to distract you from seeing
my outfit has been put together
by a mix of clothes swap and charity shop.

Who knew there was so much to pay for as an adult?

That a pension
wasn't something as far off as my own mortality?

Lidl and Aldi
have become the life blood of my existence.
My optimistic savings accounts were long ago depleted.
I now only service my car
at the tried and tested half-price garage.
I thank past selves for the unidentifiable Tupperware boxes
I once put in the freezer,
pace the house searching for possessions I can sell on eBay.
Still nobody wants a copy of *Sliding Doors* on VHS.

Artistic poverty was meant to be a rite of passage,
JK Rowling in her *Harry Potter* café.
One day they'll turn my local coffee shop
into a shrine to me,
    which would be a nice idea
        if inflation hadn't increased the price of coffee
        beyond the realms of acceptability.

Who needs disposable income when you've got
three of a five-act self-aware, yet deprecating
one-woman show mapped out in your head?

Who needs a house, a mortgage, gas and electricity,

a phone, the internet, a car and foreign holidays,
a laptop, a telly, savings for when the boiler breaks?
Who needs trainers, new clothes,
insurance against all the things that can and do go wrong,
the world's smallest but inexplicably most expensive dog

when you've got so many feelings
and the means to express them
through the power of art
and bloody well-crafted poem?

I'VE MISJUDGED THE TITLE OF THIS BOOK

As soon as the ink's dry on the page
the wind's changed.
I'm reading the final draft to my mum via Skype
while Hunt's just clarified what he really meant
by a *fairer funded NHS*.
I'm furious about fuel payments;
there are only so many words that rhyme with
means tested.
I've barely opened my mouth
at a gig
before the *Guardian*'s announcing a U-turn.

My publisher gives me a deadline of a year away.
I want to play it safe.
Pick general themes,
my mum says:
inequality,
climate change,
the divide between rich and poor.

Don't write three pages
on the finer points of the dementia tax.
Don't stick all your eggs in one basket.
Certainly don't base the next couple of years of your career
on one single Labour leader.
Imagine in 1997 if someone had written a poetry collection
entitled
Tony Blair: The Voice of Peaceful Socialism.

I'm trying to turn away from it all,
find inspiration in
the moon,
a hedgehog,
the humble street pigeon
or go back to some of my early themes:
men,
drinking,
my feelings.

Come midday I turn off
Daily Politics
in favour of *Come Dine With Me*.

Don't get swept up
with the braying social media mob
by writing my own three-minute put-down of
whatever it is that's boiled our blood
because I know that as soon as I click *upload*
the protestors will have put down their pitchforks.
It just shifts too quickly.
I can't keep up with the list of names on Yewtree,
the spiralling of the expenses scandal,
who's taken part in some humiliating initiation ceremony.

Each morning I'm checking Twitter
through gritted teeth
like the paranoid wife
of a man too honest too have cheated.

Don't let me down, Jeremy.
Don't you dare let me down.[1]

---

1   If you are reading this book at a point when Jeremy
     Corbyn has let us all down, please still recommend it
     to your friends.

INNUENDO AND HOT POT

For twenty years my 7.30s
have been low stakes,
family dinners,
snogging in the alley,
back from the dead lovers,
whirlwind weddings and adultery.
I don't want my Friday nights
to come with a trigger warning,
gird your loins before you turn the TV on.
There are only so many scenes
with crying women on the wrong side
of a locked door I can handle,
only so many first-person
handheld shaky camera angles.
How can there be so many stalkers living on one street?
I don't want to still be worrying about the fate
of Andy in the basement
the next morning over breakfast,
my early evening gentle safe place,
bookies taking bets
on whether Michelle Connor gets raped.
I don't want stabbings in the bistro,
orphaned kids,
human trafficking,
six deaths in a week.
Give me tipsy regulars,
rows over the jukebox,
auditions for the school nativity,
runaway dogs,
give me fights in the butcher's
over the price of pork chops,
give me a terraced house credit roll,
give me innuendo and hot pot.

PETER AND WILL HAVE A NEW PLAY THEY'RE VERY PROUD OF

We sit circular around them,
these two men
in their thirties.
In the itinerary
that was handed out
we were told they were meant to speak
ten minutes ago,
just before me,
but, running late,
they slipped in
just as I stood up,
their delay unexplained.
I sat down again.

I shuffle the cue cards
in my hand
back into the correct order,
mouth the words in my throat,
the ones I practised
before I left home.

You'll be on at 6.30,
just after Peter.

Peter is a writer
far more established than me
and he's here with his friend
Will the director.
Can they show you the trailer?
Turn the lights off.

Peter and Will's new play
is about rape and sexual assault.
Their trailer is
seven and a half minutes long.
Peter and Will

watch, grinning,
twelve months' work finally come to fruition,
a clip of a trip to Bradford last year,
a thanks to their sponsors
without whom
none of this would be possible.

Peter and Will
haven't misjudged this
because Peter and Will
just didn't think,
didn't picture this room
before they walked into it.

Peter and Will have assumed
that this room is filled with women
who have never felt the pressure of a brick wall,
never counted the exits,
never felt hands twice the size of theirs,
certain brands of deodorant
don't make them retch,
these are women
with jobs and partners and confidence.
These women haven't declared themselves
to Peter and Will,
their trailer
and their sponsors
without whom
none of this would be possible.

DO YOU KNOW ANY CORRS SONGS?

At some point they overtook him.
They were all together on the starting line
with mortar boards, gowns,
glasses of cheap wine.
Now his mates all own champagne bars,
have no memory
of that English degree
they cruised through a while back.
They left him behind;
he became
that clapped-out dirt car
on the *Wacky Races* track.
They're all
*well done*s,
back slaps,
a shake,
a wink
over another successful contract.
Vintage Prosecco,
upcycled furniture,
sandblasted walls,
Yes, mate,
I'll have another Nebuchadnezzar.
They're gentrified South London flats,
Barbour jackets,
ironic peaked caps.
He's still
eighteen grand down
and rising,
kicking up the dirt at the back.

They're houses with furniture
that didn't come flat pack,
brought back from Saturday slow morning markets,
hipster ironic bring and buy sales
in green belt country houses,
they're dog walks,

savings accounts,
the weekend papers
read and devoured,
not ripped up and smoked
in place of Tesco Value
cigarette roaches.

He's the writer
who sweated every gram
of frustration
out of an English degree,
kicked Beckett to the kerb
with how well
he understood
An Act Without Words,
wrote his dissertation in a week,
then came one mark off a first.
Ten years on
it still plagues him in his sleep.

He lives in the same village
with the same girl
he's been with since eighteen.
He loves Jenny.
He loves her laugh,
her smile,
how interesting she is.
The books she's read,
the things she knows,
the way she's not snobby
or a show-off
even though her head is full
of facts and news and literary quotes.

But he knows he listens less
when she talks now.
Feels a weight on his shoulders

when she suggests
they spend a weekend
home together,
wrapped up in routine,
just hanging out.

He spends the nights when she's working
with his guitar
writing poems
that fit into
four-four-paced
minor chords,
about wars against
the mainstream, mediocrity and being bored.
They drip heavy with metaphor.
It's all dark moors,
shadows across the floor,
stormy nights,
strangers at the door,
until the cat
walks past,
reminds him
with a full-pawed scratch
that it's midnight,
she hates him
and she's hungry.

There has to be more than this.

One night
the village pub next door
puts a poster up
about an open-mic.

They're trying to reinvent themselves
as a gastro place,
get over the local MP

who got caught
stuffing coke up his face
in the toilets
last week.

So he's there at six.
Some of the regulars
say, *Alright, mate, how's the Mrs?*
But he's got his guitar
and his songs.
They tell him
he can be first on;
well, until anyone else turns up,
because currently
he's the only one.

He does his pieces
about being lost and alone
and no one moans,
but most of them
have their faces
lit up
by Facebook on their phones.
He's about to give up
and just go home
when he remembers
he knows the basic tune
of *Thunder Road.*

Suddenly
there's this attention on him,
phones away,
eyes in place,
like the distant
click of a light switch.

He remembers most of the words,

nearly all of the chords.
By the time he's done
they're begging him for more.

He doesn't know any
but he promises to be back next week,
so the landlord
takes his number
and his name
because in this village
young men with guitars
and songs
you can sing along to
don't come along every day.

Next Tuesday comes,
he's back,
the room's filled with a buzz.
The open-mic sign's come down
ready for his set.

He's been practising.
My God,
has he been practising.

Forget the poetry;
he's not written one all week.
Now solely covers are his passion
and he kicks them off
with Don't Stop Believing,
then straight into some
Fleetwood Mac.
Before anyone can
escape to the loo
he's into the third verse
of *Love Shack.*
Brown Eyed Girl,
Hard Day's Night,

Common People,
500 Miles,
All Along the Watchtower,
Wuthering Heights,
Sweet Home Alabama,
Beastie Boys,
Fight for Your Right.

There are bodies
getting closer to the stage,
dancing and moving.
He can't remember
if he told Jenny
he'd be out tonight
or that he might stay for a couple.
There are these women on the dance floor,
all permed hair,
earrings in the shape of disco balls;
he knows
them from the local village magazine.
The WI are gyrating their hips,
moving to his beats.

Out of nowhere
there's this young face,
at least ten years younger than his.
It's Tuesday night
but she's dressed for the weekend.
Christ,
she looks like
she's ready
to sing Shirley Bassey hits
on a cruise liner.
All gold-sequinned
breasts and thighs,
she's looking at him,
she's hot breath in his ear,

Please can I?
a begging depth in her eyes.

Do you know any Corrs songs?
I love the Corrs.

Who loves the Corrs?

Not him.
He has no strong feelings
about the Irish quartet,
but he will for her.

Now they're singing together,
it's all
neon flashing fairy lights,
lovelorn eyes,
Do you know Summer Sunshine?
Or the one they released
for their reunion
in 2009?

He doesn't
but my God
he tries.

He gets home,
flushed and late,
humming the bridge to *Runaway*.
Jenny's waited up
to check he's OK.
He is.
He's the most OK he's been in years,
but he doesn't tell her this.
Just fakes a yawn,
puts the kettle on,
says yeah, he's great.

Then next week
he's ready,
pumped up
with hair gel,
a steady stream
of puns at his disposal.
He rocks up early
(he's been *rocking up*
to things all week),
and on his knees,
oh, thank you, God,
she's back again,
just as sequinned up
as she was last week.

So, her in her cocktail dress
and him in his suit,
they take the stage by storm.
The whole village are there,
all except one,
because they've all heard
about this schmoozing,
crooning,
guitar-playing cad
and his dolled-up beauty.

He plays the covers
she requests.
She takes his hand
on the slow songs,
mouths *you little cutie.*
He's on his knees
for his guitar riff,
looking up
at this hummingbird,
this lioness,

this nameless girl,
all hips and booty.

For an hour
they pump out
each song,
full sweated
sexual chemistry,
all thrusts and winks
and lust-locked looks
across the melody,
gyrating together
like it's just him and her alone
with this sexy background soundtrack,
not on stage
in front of the village priest,
the chicken farmer,
the milkman
and her mum and dad.
No,
they're slow and close
and the room's
in love
with it.

They finish
Yazoo,
Only You.
A roar of applause,
shouts for more.
They beg the audience
for a break.
At the bar he says,
I don't even know your name,
then she,
all bashful winks,
coy behind

giant eyelashes,
says,
I'll tell you
if you promise you're not taken.

He doesn't even pause
or wait
to make a decision.
Just says,
I'm single
free
tell me your name
and get back on that stage
beside me.

ALL THE POEMS I COULDN'T PUBLISH

will remain in boxes under my bed.

COWBOYS

It's Saturday night.
We are watching a play,
a comedy, we're told,
where a woman is assaulted
and a man
– who in real life I always quite liked –
feigns masturbation in her face.
They make her bend over
before smashing a whiskey bottle over her head.
She is wearing hot pants
which ride up as she falls to the stage.

The men cheer.
They are playing cowboys
like they are still eight years old,
still lifting up girls' skirts in the playground.

I look around at all the men
who proudly promised that with the spread of *me too*
they had had their eyes opened,
would never sit back,
never let their silence make them complicit.
They take uncomfortable sips of their pints,
don't blink,
don't turn round to their girlfriends
who have statistics running through their heads.

We leave the theatre.
No one mentions it.
Do you want a drink?
The cowboys come yee-haing from the stage door,
take selfies with the woman they just murdered.
They pose like male models on her
and she smiles.

Somebody asks for a photo
next to the sign

warning of *scenes some viewers may find upsetting.*
It's funny, isn't it?
How some people get so offended.

It's on Facebook within minutes.
It's hilarious,
their friends agree.

I'm at home on the sofa
as the likes roll in,
men – my friends –
who had sipped their pints around me,
desperate not to be the odd ones out.

WHY ALL MY SUPERSTITIONS ARE ENTIRELY FUTILE

Tapping the top
of my can of Coke
knowing it could still
explode in my face.

A LETTER OF APOLOGY TO THE LOCALS IN THE PADSTOW INN SPECIFICALLY BETWEEN THE MONTHS OF APRIL AND AUGUST

Having turned our noses up at Rick Stein's
we appear blinking
in the doorway
with our rucksacks and sunglasses,
take a window seat
near the plug socket.

I can see how much you hate us.
We really are the worst,
the kind that don't stick to Café Rouge
and Pizza Express
but go off the beaten track
in search of somewhere authentic.

We've been round every ethical jewellery
and handmade soap shop,
perused the windows of Joules and Seasalt,
successfully bought nothing
at the indoor craft market
taken the obligatory ice cream in the harbour shot.
Hold it up.

Now in your pub
gawping at the Cornish memorabilia,
putting too much effort into reading
a framed list
of all the ships insured in Padstow
in 1856,
half-heartedly writing a poem about this
and eating a freshly caught
crab salad.

ALIENS

An alien comes to earth
having spent his entire life preparing for this mission,
every night studying human behaviour
through the world of Western media advertising,
TV,
Netflix,
'skip after three seconds' YouTube clips,
billboards,
magazines,
the sides of buses,

until he decides to go for it,
crash-lands his rocket
in a field and, staggering
blinking from the wreckage,
bumps into a human who's female.
He can tell by the way she doesn't try to kill him.

He's baffled by her lack of hot pants,
her dull skin.
She doesn't seem to have any cats to feed.
She's bigger than expected,
but maybe she's about to start Weight Watchers
or eating probiotic yoghurt.
Her hair isn't as shiny as he was led to believe,
but looking around
he sees
she's probably searching for a
forest waterfall to have an orgasm in.

WE MUST BE CAREFUL NOT TO DO TO JEREMY CORBYN WHAT WE DID TO BARACK OBAMA AND PUT HIM ON A PEDESTAL FROM WHICH HE CAN ONLY BE A DISAPPOINTMENT

Jeremy Corbyn will fix my bike
Jeremy Corbyn will ease my back ache
Jeremy Corbyn will sort out my noisy neighbours
Jeremy Corbyn will remember my birthday
Jeremy Corbyn will buy me a voucher for a spa weekend
Jeremy Corbyn will ban anti-ageing cream adverts
 and the ones where women eat yoghurt in their pants
Jeremy Corbyn will raise income tax
 but only for my ex-boyfriends and then he will spend it on
 setting up a dog-friendly poetry night in the East Midlands
Jeremy Corbyn will adequately fund the arts
Jeremy Corbyn will adequately fund education
Jeremy Corbyn will adequately fund the NHS
Jeremy Corbyn will sew up all the moth holes in my favourite
 T-shirts
Jeremy Corbyn will chase up those unpaid invoices
Jeremy Corbyn will remind me to go to bed at ten
Jeremy Corbyn will suggest I don't have that last glass of red
Jeremy Corbyn will stop me getting anxious on Sunday nights
 or at any other time
Jeremy Corbyn will make the people at BBC Writersroom pick
 up my script
Jeremy Corbyn will stop men who work as accountants
 offering me constructive criticism at gigs
Jeremy Corbyn will do that for love
Jeremy Corbyn will create emerging artist programmes where
 at some point
 the artists actually emerge
Jeremy Corbyn will renationalise the railways
Jeremy Corbyn will spray my suede shoes before I wear them
 impatiently in the rain
Jeremy Corbyn will give me away at my wedding
 then lead the speeches
 the first dance

the cutting of the cake
Jeremy Corbyn will marry me
Jeremy Corbyn will finance my one-woman Edinburgh show
    portraying the life of my blind three-legged
    toy poodle, attend every performance
    and give it five stars in the *Scotsman*
Jeremy Corbyn will water my plants for me when I go away on
    holiday
Jeremy Corbyn will make Leonard Cohen immortal
Jeremy Corbyn will make Bruce Springsteen immortal
Jeremy Corbyn will make Bob Dylan immortal
    (and as good as he used to be)
Jeremy Corbyn will make me look really popular and
    successful at that social event in front of people
    I went to school with
Jeremy Corbyn will pay my gas bill
Jeremy Corbyn will pay back my start-up loan
Jeremy Corbyn will pay off my student debt
Jeremy Corbyn will successfully run a training event without
    the need of an interactive icebreaker
Jeremy Corbyn will take me on a cycling holiday around
    Croatia we will ride in tandem
Jeremy Corbyn will follow me on Twitter
Jeremy Corbyn will read this poem
Jeremy Corbyn will tell me he likes it.

ACKNOWLEDGEMENTS

Thank you to both the Conservative Party and the patriarchy, my two great sources of inspiration.

To audiences at Find The Right Words who listened to these poems as they developed.

To Taffy Grais, for cover design, illustrations and patience.

And to Dave, who continues to be the best person I've ever met.

Lightning Source UK Ltd.
Milton Keynes UK
UKHW011117170519
342860UK00001B/59/P